MARIJUANA
AFFECTING LIVES

BY JANIE HAVEMEYER

MOMENTUM

Published by The Child's World®
1980 Lookout Drive • Mankato, MN 56003-1705
800-599-READ • www.childsworld.com

Photographs ©: iStockphoto, cover, 1, 5, 15, 17, 18;
Shutterstock Images, 6, 14, 24, 28; Africa Studio/
Shutterstock Images, 8; Jon Osumi/Shutterstock
Images, 11; Andrey Popov/Shutterstock Images,
12; Aaron Amat/Shutterstock Images, 21; Monkey
Business Images/Shutterstock Images, 22; Light
Field Studios/iStockphoto, 27

ISBN 9781503844858 (Reinforced Library Binding)
ISBN 9781503846449 (Portable Document Format)
ISBN 9781503847637 (Online Multi-user eBook)
LCCN 2019957710

Printed in the United States of America

Some names and details have been changed
throughout this book to protect privacy.

CONTENTS

MOMENTUM

FAST FACTS

What It Is

► Marijuana comes from the hemp plant. Another name for hemp is **cannabis**.

► Other names for marijuana are pot, herb, weed, and grass. Stronger forms are hash and hash oil.

► THC is a chemical found in marijuana that has mind-changing effects.

How It's Used

► Marijuana is smoked. It is also put into food and eaten.

Physical Effects

► Marijuana affects each person differently.

► THC affects normal brain functions. People can have trouble learning, remembering, moving, and solving problems.

► Marijuana can affect a person's **coordination**. This can make it harder to do activities such as sports.

► Quitting marijuana may cause **withdrawal** symptoms. Symptoms include feeling anxious and cranky, having trouble sleeping, and experiencing cravings.

Effects of Heavy Marijuana Use

Teens who heavily use marijuana . . .

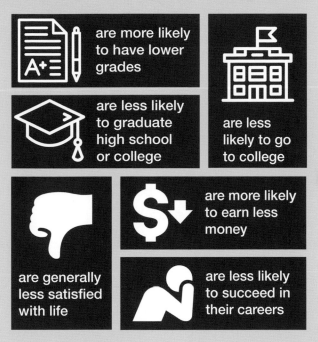

are more likely to have lower grades

are less likely to graduate high school or college

are less likely to go to college

are more likely to earn less money

are generally less satisfied with life

are less likely to succeed in their careers

"Marijuana Use and Educational Outcomes." *National Institute on Drug Abuse*, 2014, drugabuse.gov. Accessed 13 Nov. 2019.

Mental Effects

► The chemicals in marijuana affect people's moods. Long-term use can lead to feeling depressed and anxious. It can also lead to losing energy and having less interest in activities.

► Marijuana can make people imagine things that are not really there.

► If people use marijuana again and again, they may become **addicted**. They may need help to stop using it.

CHAPTER ONE

RECOGNIZING A PROBLEM

Fourteen-year-old Maya took a puff of a marijuana cigarette. She had never tried the drug before. The smoke Maya inhaled burned her lungs and made her cough, but she kept smoking.

At first, Maya smoked because she thought it made her look cool. But soon she was smoking whenever she felt nervous or sad. It became her way to escape her bad feelings. Marijuana helped her to relax. When she was **high**, she did not worry about things.

By the time Maya was 15, she was smoking every day. She played on her school's softball team, but marijuana affected the way she played. It was harder for her to catch and hit the ball. Her timing was off. She began to miss practice. She would rather be smoking anyway. Soon she started skipping classes to smoke.

◄ **Peers may pressure teenagers into trying marijuana.**

▲ **Becoming addicted to drugs such as marijuana can cause behavior changes that lead to discipline problems.**

When she failed her honors English class in the winter, she wept quietly in the school bathroom. Maya did not like the person she had become. She knew her smoking habit made it difficult to focus and concentrate. It was hard for her to learn and remember new things.

Maya promised herself she would stop smoking marijuana, but she could not stop. Teens are four to seven times more likely to get addicted to marijuana than adults are. Teenagers' brains are still developing. So if they regularly expose their brains to THC, it can change the way their brains work. This can lead to addiction.

About 25 to 50 percent of people who use marijuana every day become addicted. Maya was addicted.

One day, Maya crept outside school to get high by herself. When she tried to get back into the building, the security guard noticed her red eyes. Her clothes smelled like marijuana. The guard stopped Maya to ask her what she had been doing. She lied. But later, Maya was summoned to the principal's office. Her mother was waiting for her there, a frown on her face. Maya decided to tell them the truth because she had turned into someone she did not like.

Maya agreed to go to a treatment program to help with her marijuana addiction. She hated the program at first. But as the weeks rolled by, she began to understand how smoking marijuana was hurting her. Marijuana had numbed her bad feelings, but it had also made her care less about everything else.

FINDING HELP

There are certain programs that help marijuana users quit. Some are just for teens. They focus on counseling. They have teen support groups. Teens help each other by sharing and listening. A trusted teacher or coach can also help teens find help for themselves or a friend.

In therapy, Maya learned tools to help her fight her urge to smoke. She practiced using distracting activities. She started drawing and discovered she was good at it. She threw herself into her schoolwork. She began playing softball with the team again.

Maya's hand stung when the softball landed hard in her mitt. Now she caught the ball most of the time, unlike when she had been smoking instead of practicing. She aimed the ball straight back to the third baseman, who then tagged the player out.

Sometimes Maya felt the urge to smoke. When she did, she practiced some of the skills she learned to fight the craving. One of these was doing an activity that would distract her. So Maya sketched flowers. She was thankful she got the help she needed. She would keep on trying to fight her craving. She would not let marijuana hold her back.

With help from professionals, marijuana ▶ users can overcome addiction and find healthy activities to do instead.

CHAPTER TWO

A DRUG TEST

Jason walked into the museum in downtown Baton Rouge, Louisiana. He worked there as a temporary employee. His boss met him in the hallway with a big smile. She told Jason that they wanted to hire him as a permanent employee. Jason felt like shouting with joy. He had waited five months for this moment. He had tried hard to be the best museum tour guide. But then his boss said, "Just head over to the clinic and get the drug test out of the way. Then you will officially be a part of the team." Jason froze in place. He smoked marijuana every night to relax. In fact, he had been smoking it for 13 years—ever since he was a teenager.

Jason ducked into the bathroom on his way to the clinic. His heart was racing, and he felt sick. Jason knew that he would have to give a sample of his urine at the clinic. The clinic would find traces of THC in Jason's urine. Jason knew he would fail the test.

◀ **Many jobs require applicants to pass a drug test.**

▲ **THC can be detected in urine for up to a
month for regular marijuana smokers.**

Worst of all, he felt embarrassed. He could not face his boss when
she discovered the truth. Jason rushed home and called her. He
pretended that he had a family emergency and could not accept
the job after all.

Jason found work doing odd jobs where he knew he would not
have to take any drug tests. He felt sad and angry that his drug
habit had stolen the job he loved. When his daughter was born,
Jason decided to quit smoking marijuana. He wanted to be a
better role model for her.

Jason was **dependent** on marijuana. His body was used to
the drug. His doctor told him that stopping might be hard at first.

▲ THC from marijuana smoke can affect children.
This is one reason why some parents who
smoke quit when they have children.

He would have withdrawal symptoms. He might have trouble sleeping and eating. But Jason was determined to try. For the first five nights he could not sleep. He felt anxious and cranky, like his brain was on fire. But on the fifth day he began to feel calmer. By the eighth day the bad feelings mostly went away. Jason continued to turn away from smoking marijuana. It was hard, but the longer he did not smoke, the easier it became not to do it.

One day, Jason went to the museum to check out a new exhibit. When he passed the office where his old boss worked, he poked his head inside. She waved at him, so Jason went to greet her. She stood up to shake his hand.

"How good to see you again," she said. "We will be hiring a new tour guide next month. Are you still interested?"

"I would like that," Jason said, and he meant it. This time he would be ready to take the drug test and pass.

People who go through marijuana withdrawal may ▶ have trouble falling asleep, staying asleep, or both.

CANNABIS
CHOCOLATE
ORIGINAL AMSTERDAM
MILK CHOCOLATE WITH HEMP SEEDS AND
HAZELNUT PIECES

CANNABIS
CHOCOLATE
ORIGINAL AMSTERDAM
70% DARK CHOCOLATE WITH HEMP SEEDS
AND HAZELNUT PIECES

Mary & Juana
premium cannabis chocolate
dark
with real cannabis | 70%
made of selected finest cocoa | cocoa

real cannabis inside
CANNABIS
SPACE CAKE
coconut
PRODUCED BY MULTITRANCE

real cannabis inside
CANNABIS
SPACE CAKE
hash
PRODUCED BY MULTITRANCE

real cann
CAN
SPAC
pure
PRODUCED BY

NABIS
TE COOKIES
CHILL OUT

real cannabis inside
CANNABIS
SPACE CAKE
coconut
PRODUCED BY MULTITRANCE

real cannabis inside
CANNABIS
SPACE CAKE
hash
PRODUCED BY MULTITRANCE

real c
CA
SPA
pe
PRODUCED

E CAKE
Amsterdam
NNABIS
ATE COOKIES
CHILL OUT

real cannabis inside
CANNABIS
SPACE CAKE
coconut

real cannabis inside
CANNABIS
SPACE CAKE
hash
PRODUCED BY MULTITRANCE

re
PROD

CHAPTER THREE

TOO MUCH THC

Keith's plane touched down on the runway in Colorado. It was a clear day in June. Keith was about to start his summer job at the Denver Zoo. His cousin David had told Keith that he could live with him for the summer.

When Keith arrived at David's house, he found a house key under the doormat with a note. The note was from David. It said he would be back later. It told Keith to make himself at home and to eat anything in the refrigerator. After Keith dumped his bags in the spare room, he headed to the kitchen. First, he cooked himself a hamburger. For dessert, he grabbed a candy bar from the top shelf of the refrigerator. Its label said, "Marshmallow S'mores." Marshmallow s'mores was Keith's favorite candy flavor. But he did not notice the small, printed warning in the right-hand corner.

◄ **Marijuana can be included in candy or baked goods. Sometimes people may not see warning labels.**

The warning label read, "Contains cannabis oil." It also said to eat the bar in small doses. Keith ate the whole bar.

A little later, Keith started to feel strange. His heart pounded, and he felt sick to his stomach. He had trouble keeping his eyes open. Keith was scared. He did not understand what was happening to him. He reached for his phone to call 911. When he did, he saw a small creature with pointed ears digging into his right arm. Keith thought his body was being attacked by aliens. By now, his heart was racing so fast that he thought he was having a heart attack. Then he blacked out.

Keith woke up lying in a hospital room with a doctor staring down at him. Dr. Eric Brown was an emergency room doctor. He told Keith that he had eaten a marijuana chocolate bar. Keith had eaten six times more of the **edible** than the package advised. And he had eaten too much of it too quickly. David had found Keith moaning and crying and had called 911. Keith told the doctor about seeing a creature on his arm. The doctor explained that large doses of marijuana can trick a person's brain into imagining things. The creature had seemed real to Keith, but it was not.

Dr. Brown explained to Keith that when marijuana is eaten, it takes the body 30 minutes to two hours to feel the effects.

High heart rate, headaches, and confusion are ▶ symptoms of taking too much marijuana.

▲ **Having too much marijuana can lead to hospitalization.**

So people do not always realize that they are eating too much. Dr. Brown said that about three or four people a week come into his emergency room from eating too much marijuana in edibles. This can lead to an **overdose**. When people overdose on edible marijuana, they can feel terrible anxiety. They may also feel panic and confusion. They can imagine things and vomit.

People are more likely to overdose from eating edibles than from smoking marijuana. Overdosing from smoking marijuana is unlikely. As of 2019, no one has directly died of a marijuana overdose. For this and other reasons, some states have made marijuana use **legal**.

Keith left the hospital later that afternoon. David told him that he was sorry. He felt bad that he had left the bars in the refrigerator without warning Keith. Keith thought the chocolate bars needed bigger warning labels. He decided to write a letter to the company who sold them. He would share his story. He did not want anyone else to go through the same experience.

THE DANGERS OF EDIBLES

Some states have laws that allow people over the age of 21 to use marijuana. Because of this, marijuana products that people can eat are becoming more common. Products can look like harmless candy, such as gummy bears and lollipops. Marijuana edibles have led to an increase in people accidentally having too much marijuana. Just because marijuana is legal to use in some states, that does not make it safe.

CHAPTER FOUR

BREAKING THE LAW

Natalie slipped ten plastic baggies of marijuana into her eyeglass case. Her friend Mike had been selling marijuana to her for years. Natalie had started smoking when she was 15. Mike said she could make good money selling it. Natalie had slowly saved up money from odd jobs to buy the baggies from Mike. She imagined all the new clothes and shoes that she could buy with the money she would make selling marijuana.

A few days later, Natalie left her purse at the checkout counter in a store at the mall. She panicked when she realized it was gone. Her eyeglass case with the marijuana was inside. She ran back to the store as though she were running a race. Natalie made a dash back to the checkout counter to ask for her purse. The saleswoman gave her a hard stare and told her to wait. Natalie knew right away that something was wrong.

◀ **Even in states where marijuana is legal, sales must be made in stores that have a license.**

Thoughts whirled through her head. Natalie remembered how upset her parents had been when they found out she smoked marijuana. Her father had warned her that marijuana could damage her brain. The brain grows and forms up through a person's mid-20s. Marijuana use can change the brain's size when it is still growing. Some studies have shown that marijuana use can lower a teen's **IQ**. It can harm the way the brain functions. Over time, a teen's memory and attention can get worse. Still, Natalie had not wanted to stop. Marijuana seemed harmless. She had never heard of anyone dying from it. She lied to her parents, promising them she had quit smoking.

A big police officer approached Natalie. He had a gun at his hip. He told her he was a detective. He was taking her to the police station. Natalie realized someone had discovered the marijuana in her purse. She started to cry. People stared at her as she walked through the mall. She hung her head in shame. At the police station, she told the officer that she had planned to sell the marijuana. Her parents were quiet when they picked her up. They told her a judge would decide her punishment. Natalie had broken the law.

Two months later, Natalie went before the judge, who sentenced her to 30 days in jail. Her crime was having marijuana and planning to sell it. Natalie looked out at the courtroom.

▲ **The level of punishment for selling marijuana partly depends on state laws and the amount of marijuana the person had.**

She saw her parents and her younger sister. Some of her friends had come to support her, too. Natalie broke down and cried. She felt embarrassed.

In her jail cell, Natalie sobbed. Her sister wrote her a letter about how much she missed her. Natalie's parents were angry that she had lied. They had to take time off work to visit her.

▲ Legal punishment for selling marijuana can be much worse than for just smoking it.

Her mother cried a lot during the visits. Natalie felt terrible watching her family suffer.

Natalie sat on the hard bed in her jail cell. She had no one to blame but herself for why she was there. She vowed to change. She spent her time in jail following the rules and was released early for good behavior. When she went back to school, she avoided hanging out with smokers. She focused on her classes and her desire to go to college instead. She worked hard to gain back her parents' trust. Natalie had learned from her mistakes and set herself on a better path.

THINK ABOUT IT

► How might marijuana affect a person's performance in school and other activities?

► Marijuana addiction can hurt many parts of people's lives. Why do you think people continue to use drugs even when it has a negative impact on them?

► Why do you think some states allow people to use marijuana legally?

► What can companies do to prevent people from overeating legal marijuana products?

GLOSSARY

addicted (uh-DIK-tid): Someone who is addicted feels a very strong need to do or have something regularly. People who use marijuana can become addicted to the drug.

cannabis (KAN-uh-bus): Cannabis is another name for marijuana. The chocolate bar was made with cannabis oil.

coordination (koh-or-duh-NAY-shun): Coordination is having good control when moving different parts of the body. Marijuana can affect coordination.

dependent (di-PEN-duhnt): A person who is dependent on a drug feels a physical need to keep taking it. Jason was dependent on smoking marijuana to feel calm.

edible (EH-duh-bul): An edible is a food item made with marijuana. It is easy to take in too much marijuana when eating an edible.

high (HY): Being high on a drug means having the feeling of euphoria from taking the drug. Many people use marijuana to get high.

IQ: An IQ is a number that is used to measure a person's intelligence. A teen's marijuana use can cause his or her IQ to drop by several points.

legal (LEE-guhl): Something that is legal is allowed by the law. Marijuana use is legal for adults in some states.

overdose (OH-vur-dohss): An overdose is a dose of a drug that is too large and may either make a person sick or kill that person. A marijuana overdose can cause someone to hallucinate.

withdrawal (with-DRAW-uhl): Withdrawal is the experience of physical and mental effects when a person stops taking an addictive drug. Jason had withdrawal symptoms when he stopped using marijuana.

TO LEARN MORE

BOOKS

Alexander, Richard. *What's Drug Abuse?*
New York, NY: KidHaven Publishing, 2019.

Benson, Jodyanne. *The Dangers of Marijuana*.
New York, NY: PowerKids Press, 2020.

Paris, Stephanie Herweck. *Drugs and Alcohol*.
Huntington Beach, CA: Teacher Created Materials, 2013.

WEBSITES

Visit our website for links about addiction to
marijuana: **childsworld.com/links**

*Note to Parents, Teachers, and Librarians: We routinely verify our Web links to make
sure they are safe and active sites. So encourage your readers to check them out!*

SELECTED BIBLIOGRAPHY

Barclay, R. Sam. "Marijuana Can Be Addictive: Who Gets Hooked and
Why." *Healthline*, 2 Aug. 2019, healthline.com. Accessed 12 Nov. 2019.

Davis, Kenneth L. and Mary Jeanne Kreek. "Marijuana
Damages Young Brains." *The New York Times*, 16 June
2019, nytimes.com. Accessed 12 Nov. 2019.

"Marijuana: Facts for Teens." *National Institute on Drug Abuse*,
Dec. 2017, drugabuse.gov. Accessed 12 Nov. 2019.

INDEX

ABOUT THE AUTHOR

Janie Havemeyer is the author of many books for kids, both nonfiction and fiction. She holds a master's degree in education from Bank Street College in New York City. For many years, Janie taught in elementary schools and in art museums. She lives in San Francisco, California.